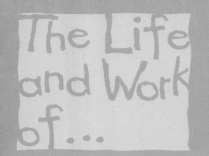

The Life and Work of...

Georges Seurat

Paul Flux

Heinemann
LIBRARY

www.heinemann.co.uk/library
Visit our website to find out more information about Heinemann Library books.

To order:
 Phone 44 (0) 1865 888066
 Send a fax to 44 (0) 1865 314091
 Visit the Heinemann Bookshop at www.heinemann.co.uk/library to browse our catalogue and order online.

First published in Great Britain by Heinemann Library, Halley Court, Jordan Hill, Oxford OX2 8EJ, a division of Reed Educational and Professional Publishing Ltd. Heinemann is a registered trademark of Reed Educational and Professional Publishing Ltd.

OXFORD MELBOURNE AUCKLAND JOHANNESBURG BLANTYRE
GABORONE IBADAN PORTSMOUTH (NH) USA CHICAGO

Designed by Celia Floyd
Illustrations by Sam Thompson
Originated by Ambassador Litho Ltd
Printed and bound in Hong Kong/China

ISBN 0 431 09219 2

06 05 04 03 02
10 9 8 7 6 5 4 3 2 1

British Library Cataloguing in Publication Data

Flux, Paul
   The life and work of Georges Seurat
   1. Seurat, Georges, 1859-1891
   2. Painters – France – Biography – Juvenile literature
   3. Painting – France – Juvenile literature
   I. Title
   II. Georges Seurat
   759.4

Acknowledgements
The Publisher would like to thank the following for permission to reproduce photographs: AFP: Ben Fathers p16; AKG Photos: p4, Musée d'Orsay, Paris pp25, 29, Courtauld Institute Galleries p27; Bridgeman Art Library: Art Institute of Chicago p17, Courtauld Gallery, London p5, National Gallery, London p15, Musée des Beaux-Arts, Tournai p21, Musée d'Orsay, Paris p18, Private Collection p11; César de Hauke: p9; Magnum Photos: p20; Metropolitan Museum of Art, New York: p7, bequest of Stephen C Clarke pp13, 23; Roger Viollet: pp6, 22, 24; Tate Picture Library: p19.

Cover photograph reproduced with permission of National Gallery, London/Bridgeman Art Library.

Every effort has been made to contact copyright holders of any material reproduced in this book.
Any omissions will be rectified in subsequent printings if notice is given to the Publisher.

Any words appearing in the text in bold, **like this**, are explained in the Glossary.

Contents

Who was Georges Seurat?

Georges Seurat was one of the finest French artists. He lived more than 100 years ago. People today still enjoy his pictures of the people and places he knew.

Georges invented a new way of painting which used tiny dots of colour. The dots worked together to make the new, brighter colours he wanted in his pictures.

The Bridge at Courbevoie, 1886

Early years

Georges Seurat was born in Paris on 2 December 1859. The family home was near the Parc des Buttes-Chaumont. He showed the park in some of his paintings.

Man Leaning on a Parapet, 1881–83

Georges returned to Paris in 1880. He painted this picture of a person leaning on a bridge over the River Seine. People by the river became one of Georges' favourite **subjects**.

A special exhibition

In 1883, when he was 23, Georges had a painting shown at the **Salon**. This was a special **exhibition** in Paris where the best artists showed their work. This was a great honour for Georges.

This is the picture Georges had shown at the Salon. It is a drawing of his close friend Aman-Jean. This was the only painting Georges had at the Salon in his whole lifetime!

Portrait of Aman-Jean, 1883

Painting with dots

In the spring of 1883 Georges began his first large painting. It showed bathers in water. This was not chosen to be shown at the 1884 **Salon**. Rejected paintings were shown in their own **exhibition**. Georges' picture was hung in the canteen!

Bathers at Asnières, 1883–84

In *Bathers at Asnières*, Georges showed how colour could be used in a new way. He painted with small dots. The dots mix together in the viewer's eye to make all the different colours of the painting.

The modern painter

In the winter of 1884 and 1885 Georges worked on another large painting. It was of an island in the River Seine, called La Grande Jatte. In the 1880s it was a very popular place for people to walk.

When the painting was shown many people did not like it. They thought a picture of people walking by the river was not a good **subject** for a large painting.

Sunday Afternoon at La Grande Jatte, 1884–86

Growing fame

After he painted *La Grande Jatte*, Georges became better known. Other artists began to copy his way of painting. This picture is by Paul Signac. He and Georges became very close friends.

Le Bec du Hoc, Grandcamp, 1885

In the summer of 1885 Georges stayed in the
town of Grandcamp in Normandy. The town is
on the **coast** of France. He wanted his paintings
to show what the sea really looked like there.

19

To catch the moment

Georges spent the next summer in the **coastal** town of Honfleur. He still wanted to paint pictures of light, water and the sea-shore. Georges worked outside to get his colours as **accurate** as possible.

Shore at Bas Butin, Honfleur, 1886

This is one of the pictures Georges painted at Honfleur. Many other artists also began to paint with dots like Georges. This way of painting is now known as **pointillism**.

Mystery of the circus

Some people said that Georges could only paint **landscapes**. So he looked for something to paint in which people were important. He chose the circus, a very popular show in Paris.

Invitation to the Sideshow, 1887–88

Georges often visited the Circus Corvi in Paris. People at the circus are usually happy. Georges did not show them having fun in this picture. He has used dark colours to show sadness.

An ordinary life

In 1888 Georges spent his summer at Port-en-Bessin, on the French **coast**. He did many drawings and **sketches** which he used later in his paintings. He seemed very happy.

Georges painted six pictures of Port-en-Bessin that summer. He liked the peace and stillness. He tried to show this in his paintings.

Port-en-Bessin, 1888

Love and a family

In 1889 Georges met and fell in love with Madeleine Knobloch. They lived together in Georges' art **studio**. In February 1890 they had a son, whom they called Pierre Georges.

Young Woman Powdering Herself, 1890

This is the only large **portrait** that Georges ever painted. It shows Madeleine in front of a mirror, putting on make-up.

Final days

On 29 March 1891 Georges died suddenly of **meningitis**. He was just 31. His son died a short time later of the same disease.

This was the last painting Georges worked on. He had not finished it when he died. Georges is famous for his paintings which made ordinary people and things seem special.

The Circus,
1891

Timeline

1859	Georges Seurat is born in Paris on 2 December.
1878	Georges joins the Paris School of Fine Art.
1879	He spends one year in the army.
1880	He returns to live in Paris.
1883	Georges has his first picture shown at the **Salon**.
	He begins to paint *Bathers at Asnières*.
1884	Georges helps start the Society of Independent Artists.
1886	He shows his paintings at the **Impressionist exhibition**.
	He finishes *Sunday Afternoon at La Grande Jatte*.
1887	He shows his paintings with the Belgian artists, 'The Twenty'.
1888	Georges spends the summer painting at Port-en-Bessin on the **coast**.
	He finishes *Invitation to the Sideshow*.
1889	He meets Madeleine Knobloch and lives with her at his **studio**.
1890	Georges and Madeleine have a son, Pierre Georges.
	Georges spends the summer painting at Gravelines, on the coast.
1891	Georges dies suddenly from **meningitis** in Paris on March 29.

Glossary

accurate   as near true as possible

coast   where the land meets the sea

encourage   to persuade someone to do something

exhibition   works of art on display for people to see

Impressionists   group of artists who showed the effect of light and movement in their pictures

landscape   picture of the countryside

meningitis   disease that affects the brain and causes headaches and high temperature

Old Masters   great artists from Europe who lived a long time ago

pointillism   way of painting using tiny dots of colour

portrait   picture of a person

Salon   France's official art exhibition which was held every year

sketch   unfinished or rough drawing or painting

studio   special room or building where an artist works

subject   something shown in a painting

More books to read

How Artists Use Colour, Paul Flux, Heinemann Library

More paintings to see

The Beach at Gravelines, Georges Seurat, Courtauld Institute of Art, London

House Among Trees, Georges Seurat, City Art Gallery, Glasgow

Man Painting a Boat, Georges Seurat, Courtauld Institute of Art, London

Rue Saint-Vincent, Montmartre, in Spring, Georges Seurat, Fitzwilliam Museum, Cambridge

Index

Titles in the *Life and Work of* series include:

Hardback   0 431 09210 9

Hardback   0 431 09216 8

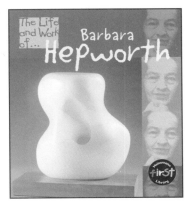

Hardback   0 431 09212 5

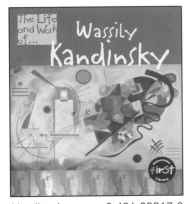

Hardback   0 431 09217 6

Hardback   0 431 09218 4

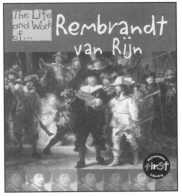

Hardback   0 431 09211 7

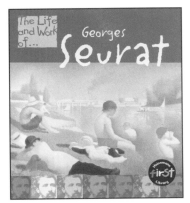

Hardback   0 431 09219 2

Find out about the other titles in this series on our website www.heinemann.co.uk/library